Simple Planners and Journals

For Busy People Like You

This book is copyright protected. Please do not reproduce in either electronic means or in printed format except for your explicit personal use. This means that copying this book is prohibited and not allowed without permission from the author. All Rights Reserved

Trip Index

Place	Date	Page

Trip Index

Place	Date	Page

Fun Things I Want To Do On This Trip

1. _____
2. _____
3. _____
4. _____
5. _____

6. _____
7. _____
8. _____
9. _____
10. _____

Fun Places I Want To See On This Trip

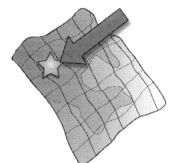

1. _____
2. _____
3. _____
4. _____
5. _____
6. _____
7. _____
8. _____
9. _____
10. _____

Books To Read On The Trip

Title	Author	Read

Books To Read On The Trip

Title	Author	Read

Notes

My Day at _____

Date: _____

The first thing I did when I got here was ...

_____

_____

What I enjoyed most here was ...

_____

_____

The most perfect part of my day was...

_____

_____

Weather 	Who Else Came with?
Favorite Foods I Ate 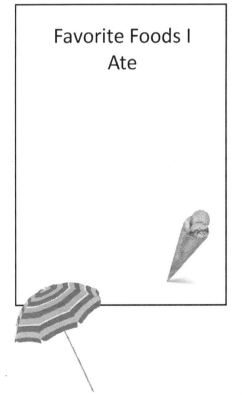	What I'll Remember Most

Doodle or Drawing about my day:

Notes

My Trip to _____

Date: _____

The name of the place we went to is …

_____

What was the best thing there? What made it so great?

_____

_____

What was the most fun part of the day?

_____

_____

Who else came with us for this trip?

Weather	Who Else Came with?
☀️ ⛅ ⛈️ 🌧️	

Favorite Foods I Ate	What I'll Remember Most

Doodle or Drawing about my day:

Notes

My Day at _____

Date: _____

The first thing I did when I got here was...

_____

_____

My 3 favorite things I saw were ...

_____

_____

Something that made me laugh was ...

_____

_____

Weather 	Who Else Came with?
Favorite Foods I Ate 	What I'll Remember Most

Doodle or Drawing about my day:

Notes

My Day at _____

Date: _____

The first thing I did when I got here was …

_____

_____

What I enjoyed most here was …

_____

_____

The most perfect part of my day was…

_____

_____

Weather 	Who Else Came with?
Favorite Foods I Ate 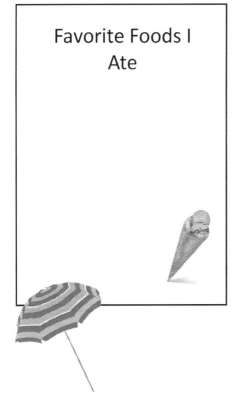	What I'll Remember Most

Doodle or Drawing about my day:

Notes

My Trip to _____

Date: _____

The name of the place we went to is …
_____

What was the best thing there? What made it so great?
_____
_____

What was the most fun part of the day?
_____
_____

Who else came with us for this trip?

Weather	Who Else Came with?
Favorite Foods I Ate	What I'll Remember Most

Doodle or Drawing about my day:

Notes

My Day at _____

Date: _____

The first thing I did when I got here was...
_____
_____

My 3 favorite things I saw were ...
_____
_____

Something that made me laugh was ...
_____
_____

Weather	Who Else Came with?

Favorite Foods I Ate	What I'll Remember Most

Doodle or Drawing about my day:

Notes

My Day at _____

Date: _____

The first thing I did when I got here was …

_____

_____

What I enjoyed most here was …

_____

_____

The most perfect part of my day was…

_____

_____

Weather 	Who Else Came with?
Favorite Foods I Ate 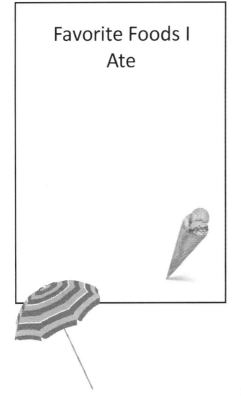	What I'll Remember Most

Doodle or Drawing about my day:

Notes

My Trip to _____

Date: _____

The name of the place we went to is ...
_____

What was the best thing there? What made it so great?
_____
_____

What was the most fun part of the day?
_____
_____

Who else came with us for this trip?

Weather	Who Else Came with?
Favorite Foods I Ate	What I'll Remember Most

Doodle or Drawing about my day:

Notes

My Day at _____

Date: _____

The first thing I did when I got here was…

_____

_____

My 3 favorite things I saw were …

_____

_____

Something that made me laugh was …

_____

_____

Weather 	Who Else Came with?
Favorite Foods I Ate 	What I'll Remember Most

Doodle or Drawing about my day:

Notes

My Day at _____

Date: _____

The first thing I did when I got here was …

_____

_____

What I enjoyed most here was …

_____

_____

The most perfect part of my day was…

_____

_____

Weather

Who Else Came with?

Favorite Foods I Ate

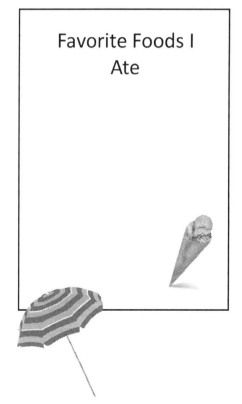

What I'll Remember Most

Doodle or Drawing about my day:

Notes

My Trip to _____

Date: _____

The name of the place we went to is ...
_____

What was the best thing there? What made it so great?
_____
_____

What was the most fun part of the day?
_____
_____

Who else came with us for this trip?

Weather 	Who Else Came with?
Favorite Foods I Ate 	What I'll Remember Most

Doodle or Drawing about my day:

Notes

My Day at _____

Date: _____

The first thing I did when I got here was…

_____

_____

My 3 favorite things I saw were …

_____

_____

Something that made me laugh was …

_____

_____

Weather 	Who Else Came with?
Favorite Foods I Ate 	What I'll Remember Most

Doodle or Drawing about my day:

Notes

My Day at _____

Date: _____

The first thing I did when I got here was …
_____
_____

What I enjoyed most here was …
_____
_____

The most perfect part of my day was…
_____
_____

Weather 	Who Else Came with?
Favorite Foods I Ate 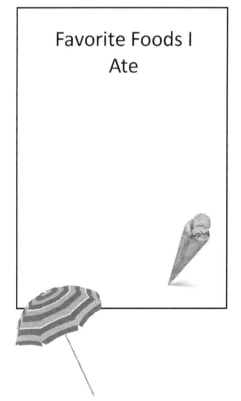	What I'll Remember Most

Doodle or Drawing about my day:

Notes

My Trip to _____

Date: _____

The name of the place we went to is ...
_____

What was the best thing there? What made it so great?
_____
_____

What was the most fun part of the day?
_____
_____

Who else came with us for this trip?

Weather	Who Else Came with?
Favorite Foods I Ate	What I'll Remember Most

Doodle or Drawing about my day:

Notes

My Day at _____

Date: _____

The first thing I did when I got here was...
_____
_____

My 3 favorite things I saw were ...
_____
_____

Something that made me laugh was ...
_____
_____

Weather	Who Else Came with?
Favorite Foods I Ate	What I'll Remember Most

Doodle or Drawing about my day:

Notes

My Day at _____

Date: _____

The first thing I did when I got here was …

_____

_____

What I enjoyed most here was …

_____

_____

The most perfect part of my day was…

_____

_____

Weather 	Who Else Came with?
Favorite Foods I Ate 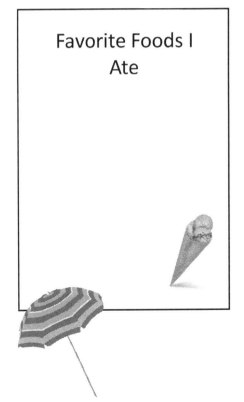	What I'll Remember Most

Doodle or Drawing about my day:

Notes

My Trip to _____

Date: _____

The name of the place we went to is ...
_____

What was the best thing there? What made it so great?
_____
_____

What was the most fun part of the day?
_____
_____

Who else came with us for this trip?

Weather	Who Else Came with?
Favorite Foods I Ate	What I'll Remember Most

Doodle or Drawing about my day:

Notes

My Day at _____

Date: _____

The first thing I did when I got here was…

_____

_____

My 3 favorite things I saw were …

_____

_____

Something that made me laugh was …

_____

_____

Weather 	Who Else Came with?
Favorite Foods I Ate 	What I'll Remember Most

Doodle or Drawing about my day:

Notes

My Day at _____

Date: _____

The first thing I did when I got here was ...
_____
_____

What I enjoyed most here was ...
_____
_____

The most perfect part of my day was...
_____
_____

Weather 	Who Else Came with?
Favorite Foods I Ate 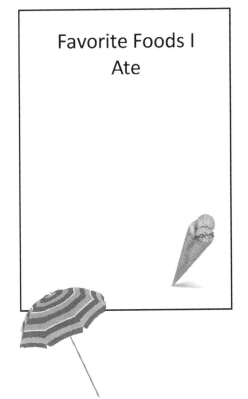	What I'll Remember Most  

Doodle or Drawing about my day:

Notes

My Trip to _____

Date: _____

The name of the place we went to is ...

What was the best thing there? What made it so great?

What was the most fun part of the day?

Who else came with us for this trip?

Weather 	Who Else Came with?
Favorite Foods I Ate 	What I'll Remember Most 

Doodle or Drawing about my day:

Notes

My Day at _____

Date: ―――――――――

The first thing I did when I got here was...

_____

_____

My 3 favorite things I saw were ...

_____

_____

Something that made me laugh was ...

_____

_____

Weather	Who Else Came with?

Favorite Foods I Ate	What I'll Remember Most

Doodle or Drawing about my day:

Notes

My Day at _____

Date: _____

The first thing I did when I got here was ...

_____

_____

What I enjoyed most here was ...

_____

_____

The most perfect part of my day was...

_____

_____

Weather 	Who Else Came with?
Favorite Foods I Ate	What I'll Remember Most

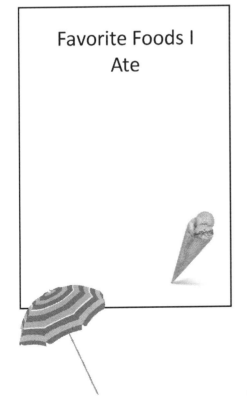

Doodle or Drawing about my day:

Notes

My Trip to _____

Date: _____

The name of the place we went to is ...
_____

What was the best thing there? What made it so great?
_____
_____

What was the most fun part of the day?
_____
_____

Who else came with us for this trip?

Weather	Who Else Came with?
Favorite Foods I Ate	What I'll Remember Most

Doodle or Drawing about my day:

Notes

My Day at _____

Date: _____

The first thing I did when I got here was...
_____
_____

My 3 favorite things I saw were ...
_____
_____

Something that made me laugh was ...
_____
_____

Weather	Who Else Came with?

Favorite Foods I Ate	What I'll Remember Most

Doodle or Drawing about my day:

Notes

Date - July. 6th.

1) November & December
   ↳ have skills to do it
   Time is the resource that we don't
2) have.

   - ability to have dedicated time
   - priority from top
   - project planning

   - maybe other depts could support the work.

What I Did: Final Thoughts

Notes

July 6th

Era - communication w/ Darcece is not good

Lucas July 7th

Notes

- Communication w/ Lisa.
- Did you/she hear me?
- I'm aware that I struggle w/ communication in the past → I don't want to be the same of it.
- clarity / wasted time.

△ improved trust, working more effectively.
△ strategic work, inefficiency, engagement.

(Strengths)

* motivational speaker
* personable / kind.
* politics of business, savvy, motivates others
* good visionary

✱✱✱✱✱✱✱✱✱✱

* weakness → Bad at compromise.

Notes

- very affected by shiny objects
- lots of data & analysis

Notes

Lorne – July 6th

Notes

Notes

Notes

Notes

Notes

Notes

Notes

Notes

Notes

Notes

Notes

Notes

Notes

Notes

Simple Planners and Journals
For Busy People Like You
Time to head to Amazon To Order Another Book
If you found this book helpful we hope that you will share that
By leaving a review on Amazon.

Manufactured by Amazon.ca
Bolton, ON

26619983R00072